Your Move into the World of Work

Your checklist for employment

By

Edward J. Kelly

authorHOUSE™

1663 LIBERTY DRIVE, SUITE 200
BLOOMINGTON, INDIANA 47403
(800) 839-8640
WWW.AUTHORHOUSE.COM

First published by AuthorHouse 08/05/04

ISBN: 1-4184-8341-9 (sc)

Printed in the United States of America
Bloomington, Indiana

This book is printed on acid-free paper.

AUTHOR'S ACKNOWLEDGMENTS

I am indebted to my staff for their help, suggestions and encouragement in assembling the original book in 1988. The Wayne County (NC) Personnel Officers Association provided input and feedback while two of their senior members, Bob Stoffel and Fred Benedict, whose combined 80 years of business experience, gave very critical reviews and comments that were incorporated into this book. A special thanks for Dr. Wayne Hatcher, Campbell University, for a final review.

Good luck to you the job hunter, as you make your move into the world of work. I hope this simplification provided by this workbook will allow for an easy transition into a job whether it is from school, unemployment, downsizing or a change of careers. Comments or suggestions are solicited and should be sent to the author at:

Ed Kelly
EK26266
edphylkelly@earthlink.net

TABLE OF CONTENTS

Chapter I
INTRODUCTION

What is the world of work really like? It is you working for a living in a place where your employer will guarantee you a paycheck and a safe environment to work. That is all that an employer is required to do. You must make the difference by your positive attitude towards the particular job and career that you have chosen.

Your attitude is going to be affected by the type of work or field of study that you choose. In this area, you need to do plenty of research to make sure you have picked the field that is right for you; not what your parents or anyone else wants, but what you want. Most people have difficulty with this selection process, but there are many resources available to you that you can draw on to assist you. The State Employment Office and the One Stop Career Centers offer free aptitude and preference testing which can assist you in exploring career areas that you would like to do and can do. College Placement Centers and other

Career Centers near you may offer the same service. Once you have your choices narrowed down, it is important that you research the occupation to find out the job description, the training that is required to do the job, the outlook for employment and the salary range. This can be accomplished in a college career center, a one-stop center or in a public or private library. The U.S. Department of Labor "Occupational Outlook Handbook" is an excellent source for this information. This is the first part of goal setting during the occupational search.

GOAL SETTING

Goal setting will never happen unless you put the goals on paper and proceed with an action response. Jim wants to be a television repairman. That's Jim's long range goal, but how does he get there? He writes them down on paper, or if so blessed he/she can put it in their computer.

GOAL ACTION
TV Repairman Two Year Associate Degree
Where: Local Community College
When: ASAP
Obstacle:
- Car Payment
- Insurance
- Tuition

You have to list obstacles in order to strategize properly. The obstacles require that sub-goals or short range goals be set. The two-year program in college may now require that the courses be taken over a three-or-four year span while Jim works part time. Hopefully after a year or two in the school program, Jim will be able to obtain a job in the TV repair field where he can obtain experience and apply what he has learned in the classroom (Cooperative Education). Let's look at Jim's plan of action now.

Goal
TV Repairman (Long Term)

Action
- Two Year Associate Degree in Electronics

Goal
- Part Time Job

Action
- Job Development
- Register ESC/JobLink/One Stop
- Check with Friends & Relatives
  (Extensive Job Development will be covered in a later chapter.)

Goal
- Register for School (short-term)

Action
- Application and Schedule completed.
- Apply for Financial Aid

Goal
- Cooperative Education Program

Action
- Maintain good grades and apply for a Co-op position

All of these looks great on paper, but something new has been added to get it all accomplished in the next three to four years, Time Management.

TIME MANAGEMENT

Time Management is you managing your life effectively. You must consider all of the known activities that you have to do, such as school, study, work and recreation. The latter is important to help you maintain your positive attitude that will keep you mentally and physically healthy. As you set mini-goals for completion of term papers and the like during a semester or quarter cycle, you are keeping your anxiety level low thereby cutting out any onslaught of depression. This is why Time Management is necessary. Plan for three months to a year and then finalize the next week's plan every Friday so you can accomplish the maximum that you can handle. Make yourself a form that has the hours in a column on the left from 6 AM until midnight. Go across the top with the days of the week from Sunday through Saturday. Put in **all** of your activities.

A possible 112 hours of useful time is available to an individual that gets eight hours of sleep per night. Shopping, etc. can come in the unscheduled hours or as part of your R & R (Rest and Relaxation) if it falls in that category. You also have time for volunteer activities that will be mentioned later under Job Development. Your plan is the plan for your life and it will only be as good as the effort you put into it. Time Management will be extremely important all of your life, but will have added emphasis when you have completed your degree and you are looking for the first career opportunity.

Chapter II
EMPLOYER
EXPECTATIONS

What are the employers looking for? First, you must have the basic entry level skills for the job you are applying for. Don't waste their time and your time by applying if you don't have these skills. Most want experience and this is where Cooperative Education can give you the cutting edge in the world of work today.

The number one trait that is desired by employers is honesty, the ability to refrain from lying, cheating or stealing and to be dependable. It has been estimated that up to twenty cents of every dollar spent today is to cover the dishonesty factor in the world of work. If you have fallen stray in your youth, you would want to check with your clerk of courts to see if your record has been closed; if not, you must be honest on your application and describe the incident. Even felons back in society can be bonded (insured for handling money) by a special program established under the State Employment Office or the One-Stop Centers.

Employers want reliable employees. They want them at work every day and also on time. What if you were a member of a 12-person team and you came in 10 minutes late? You all are making $8 an hour. You just cost your employer $16 because the others couldn't start without you. How long do you think an employer will tolerate this tardiness? Maybe twice, but the third time you would more than likely be issued your pink slip. Employers are in business to make money.

Many companies have a sick leave policy so that you will continue to draw a paycheck. It is not supposed to be used for slight colds, headaches, etc. Most employers would agree that anything over 3 days of sick leave used per year would be excessive unless it was a major medical problem. In most cases, sick leave can be accumulated and used for earlier retirement. Employers like people that can get along well with people and work on a team utilizing many of the Total Quality Management (TQM) practices. This would include those we work for, those we work with and those that work for us. If you are happy with the career you have chosen for yourself and continue to set goals to be accomplished on the job as well as in your personal life, chances are good that your positive attitude will continue to grow and you will get along well with others on the job. Remember that the only person that you can change in this life is yourself and if things are not going well at work, home, or both, you need to look first at yourself and then make the necessary changes.

You must be able to accept and handle responsibility in the world of work. You must be accountable for what you have been asked to do and you must accomplish the task with minimum supervision. You must also accept the fact that you will have to continue upgrading your skills through Continuing Education. This education or training is an investment by your company in you to make you a better employee. Continuing Education can be accomplished through special seminars, Community Colleges, or Universities. The communication skills are an utmost necessity. Being able to read and write is critical. You must be able to listen effectively and communicate orally. Any classes, workshops, etc. that you find to increase your ability in these areas, will help you in the pyramid of the world of work.

In the high tech world that we live in today, industry wants basic mathematics such as multiplication, division, percentages, averaging, and ratios used in statistics. These basic math skills are required to understand and operate in a business that has an established Quality Control System and is operating in a global economy.

Politics exists in any office, even in well-run organizations. It is important to find out whom that someone is that keeps the boss "informed" and then be extremely careful in your conversations with that individual. Of course, being a positive person, you wouldn't have anything bad to say about a person or situation.

Personnel Officers will tell you they spend 90% of their time with less than 5% of their people in trying to help them solve problems. Don't become one of the

5%. Learn to solve your own problems or leave them at home when you depart for work.

We have identified our skills or our need for training. We know what employers are looking for. Now we have to prepare ourselves and then find those jobs.

Chapter III
THE APPLICATION

The application is the "first test" of a company. It is a test of your ability to spell, write legibly, and to answer factual questions rapidly and accurately. The length of application forms vary from a "3X5" mini-application to several pages of information. The longer forms allow for much more information and generally will discourage the casual applicant.

You should have a master application completed in order that the information you have on your past history is complete and correct to the best of your ability. All blocks need to be filled in even if it is a dash or a N/A (not applicable). There never appears to be enough room to write all the information in the address blocks, but if you mentally divide the block two or three times, it will fit. It is also helpful if you don't print well to use a small straight edge to align the top of your letters as you print.

Acceptable reasons for leaving jobs are: need more hours, better pay, more challenging work, chance for advancement, moved, start school, or summer job. Unacceptable is being fired. Use the term personal and be able to explain it extremely well in the interview.

Be careful when filling out the health portion of an application. Your health is always excellent. It is illegal to ask questions relating to the past on your medical history. The question you need to ask yourself is: "Do I have anything that would affect me on this job right now?" Disabilities are covered by the Americans with Disabilities Act (ADA) which requires Employers to make necessary accommodations for the particular disability.

There are blocks on most applications that are for company use only. Do not put anything in these block/ or blocks on an application.

On the application is the request for references. You should have a minimum of three individuals that have known you well and will give you a good reference. You must personally check with each one of them to get their permission to use them as references. Do not use your analyst or any other person that is a member of a helping profession and is helping you. Don't use your banker, if your account has errors caused by you. Don't use instructors whose classes you have not been strong in. Also do not use relatives. The best are past employers who can speak well of you. You live by the record you build: dependability, minimum absenteeism, acceptable behavior, a team player, and a positive attitude.

Make sure that you include any activities that show teamwork and leadership. In some way, you must get this into your application. If hobbies are asked for, use the action ones instead of TV watching and reading. If you are an avid technical data reader, that would be acceptable.

Don't cut yourself out of a job because the application asks about travel. Get all the facts during the interview. Travel could mean one trip per month conducted all within one workday. The company will generally pay all expenses. Many trips are conferences to first class resort facilities to help you upgrade your skills. They could in this case be looked at as a "perk" or an additional benefit of the company.

The job that you are applying for will usually tell in the description whether relocation, a physical move, is required as part of the condition for employment. If this is not in the description, but is asked on the application, then we can assume that this is an informational question for later use. As your situation changes with the company after a period of time so could your attitude toward relocation. Lets look at an example. You started in Honky-tonk, North Carolina with a Fortune 500 Company in 1999 and have risen to the top of the pyramid in your occupation at that same site by 2003.

There is a position for which you are qualified with the same company in Atlanta. The new position would pay $10 K more per year and all moving expenses including pre-employment trips to Atlanta to find suitable housing. The company will even buy your house after it has been on the real-estate market for thirty days. It is decision time. Would you relocate? Only you, in consultation with your family can make that decision. The company also leaves you the option of staying in Honky-tonk. In most cases, you will not be let go by not accepting the promotion, but it could hurt your future chances for a promotion.

In summary the application is the first test of the company. It must be neat and accurate. Keep it positive and allow it to portray you in the best possible light. Show all of your leadership abilities and skills. Sell yourself.

Chapter IV
THE RESUME

There is no formula for the perfect resume. Your resume should reflect you in the most positive image you can portray on paper. In the world of e-mail, it will show you on a computer screen. Whether it is a functional or chronological resume, or a combination of both, it needs to be brief with no full sentences. It should highlight your accomplishments that will include work, education, volunteerism, honors received and special skills and abilities. All career centers and libraries have the latest books giving examples of the most acceptable resumes currently in use. Also many computer programs have excellent resumes that allow you to fine tune for any position.

The chronological is probably the one you are most familiar with. It has a heading placed in the middle of the paper to prevent it from being covered up by a routing sheet used in many personnel offices. The career objective is specific and does not keep the personnel department wondering what the individual is looking for. The career objective is generally a combination of your short and long term goals, however with today's computer resumes; it can easily be tailored to a specific company. The education is fully explained as well as the work history. There are no gaps (periods of inactivity) in either work or school. Had there been gaps the functional resume could have assisted in covering some of this up. However, you must have clear reasons for these gaps in this day and age. An interviewer will be checking to see if it was a stay in jail or a dry out from drugs or alcohol. You are building your resume and will add to it as experience and education accumulates. To keep from changing the resume often, it is suggested that you use references available on request or leave them off the resume completely. You should always have three references available on a 3X5 card tucked away where they are immediately available. Personal data that would include birth date, health, etc., are not recommended on any resume. It could be a very negative factor if you are over 40, even though by federal law, it is not supposed to be.

The functional resume looks at your strengths, experience, abilities and skills with specific examples to support each one. The "Dictionary of Occupational Titles" will tell you the specific skills that are needed for a particular job. One example for leadership could be:

Leadership - Supervised 120 individuals in a combined effort of diverse operations that received superior accolades from the CEO.

Can you put a specific example for each from this list of words?

Competent	Author
Organized	Broad Knowledge
Motivated	Generalist
Effective	Extensive
Responsible	Comprehensive
Coordinator	Communicator
Manager	Analyze
Achiever	Schedule
Punctual	Initiate
Motivator	Coordinator
Trainer	Promoter
Supervisor	

This would be the basis of your functional resume. You would start with a career objective and then use areas of accomplishments citing the specific strength or skill. In this resume, you could wrap it up with positive personal characteristics that were not used in the body of the resume. More than likely this will be the style of your Internet resume. Accomplishments are what employers are looking for so don't be modest. Tell it like it really was.

Another option is to combine both types of resumes using the functional parts to highlight strengths during the work portion and the chronological parts for school and volunteer activities. You can always fill gaps with volunteer activities.

The one things that is critical that goes with the resume is the cover letter. This needs to be addressed to a specific individual rather than a Dear Sir or Madam approach. Researching this information is covered under Job Development. If possible, the type should be the same as your resume. This is a simple three-paragraph letter that needs the same accuracy as your resume.

The first paragraph simply states that you have enclosed the resume in response to a conversation, an ad, a job order or as part of a job search. The second paragraph will state your talents that are specific to that particular company. The third paragraph will discuss your interest in an interview and that you will call his/her secretary on a specific date and time to see if an interview is arranged. Many job counselors advocate letting the employer call you, but it really shows more eagerness on your part if you initiate the call. Don't forget that the telephone contact can be part of an interview so you need to be prepared and sound pleasant and positive on the telephone. Practice until you are perfect. Use a script if necessary.

Your resume should reflect you and serve as your marketing tool to get that interview. It needs to be perfect so spend the time necessary to get it that way. The cover letter always accompanies the resume and is always addressed to a specific individual. The distribution of both will be discussed in Chapter V.

Chapter V
JOB DEVELOPMENT

I'll look in the newspapers and find a job opportunity in the Ad section. Possibly, but very few jobs are advertised. Job-hunting is a full-time business if you are unemployed. If you are employed, and looking for another job, it is strictly confidential and extracurricular to your present job.

Newspapers do offer possibilities. Jobs are created by only two things, growth and replacement. This will be important in the job search. The Business sections of a newspaper will show growth as well as job promotions, which are part of the replacement concept. Promotions should open a position some place in the company. Another good place to look in the newspaper is the Obituary section. If the individual was working when they died, the past employer is generally mentioned.

One of the first steps you need to take while job hunting is to your State Employment Office. In some locations this will now be the One Stop Center or JobLink Career Center. These Centers lists job opportunities, list job seekers, do testing for counseling purposes and merit register listings, handle unemployment insurance (UI) claims (you must have worked to draw UI benefits that have been paid by the employer), compile the Labor Market report and conduct courts to determine eligibility for unemployment insurance. This is a free service to you in any office in the land.

These Centers lists jobs by a nine-digit number called a DOT code. This number is extracted from "The Dictionary of Occupational Titles" which lists over 20,000 jobs with the DOT code. When you register at the Center, you can sign up for three different DOT codes if you are qualified. You can easily check for jobs on the computers available to the public in the center or on line from home, or you can phone in daily through the Job Information System to check for new listings. For this system you will need a touch-tone phone, your social security number, and a pin number that you assign yourself on your first call in. The center can also leave messages on this system to advise you of appointments, etc.

Direct contact with business is frustrating and expensive. Many industries today have security forces, which keep visitors out. There may be a sign that states that applications are only accepted through the State Employment Office or One Stop Center. They may tell you to write for an application or the remote possibility exists that the guard at the gate will give you an application. Nevertheless you have wasted a lot of time and incurred a great deal of travel expense when you can least afford it.

Direct contact with industry by computer on line has become the rage. Most companies have their own WEB page and many will include employment opportunities. My favorite Meta search machine is http://www.dogpile.com. Enter jobs, employment, etc, and you will get a wealth of information that you can apply with. Much of the information on the WEB pages can serve as your research on the company. Applications that are available on the Internet can either be saved or copied and pasted to your own files. In this way you can type a neat application. Watch out for those organizations that want to charge for their services.

Private employment agencies are available but they do charge a fee in most cases. Be extremely cautious and read everything before signing a contract. The Temporary agencies are the fastest growing employers in America. Twenty years ago General Motors was the world's number one employer. Manpower now holds that distinction and it is a temporary staffing agency. They get ten-week contracts with an employer for every job imaginable from sweeper to executive. At the end of the ten weeks the employer can put you on their roles if you worked out. Prior to the end of the contract, they would have to buy out the temp agency. This is not likely to happen, as this can be a large expense. While working this way you are an employee of the temporary staffing agency. They did the job development to find the job and they charge the company a set amount for your services as well as their overhead and their profit. Many companies are into this method as it gives them an excellent opportunity to see how you will work out. It is allot easier than hiring you out right and then having to build a case to fire you. It is also ideal for a person that does not want to work full time and enjoys a variety of jobs and different locations.

When looking for a job, let every friend, relative, counselor, teacher and Cooperative Education person know that you are looking for a job. This type of networking has paid handsome rewards for the job seeker. You can also use the trade, professional or industry publications in your local library. These are good for finding overseas jobs in exotic places.

The best method for finding jobs is the Direct Mail Contact. The effectiveness rate is 47.7% (Bolles 1987). This method may be changing as the computer and the Internet has had a profound effect on employment over the past few years. Direct mail is also one of the hardest because you have to prepare yourself for a great deal of research and then you have to practice meticulous time management. For local job opportunities, you can utilize the Chamber of Commerce listings combined with the yellow pages of the phone book to get a list put together of places that you would like to work that could use your particular skills. For listings in the yellow pages, you might have to make an informational telephone call to find out who the hiring authority is. If you are going to use state or regional level job development, "Standard and Poor's Register of Corporations, Directors and Executives," found in your library, will list key executives for 32,000 leading companies. At this time you need to start a 3" X 5" card file on each industry. Include the Industry name, address and telephone number along with the name of the hiring authority, product line, and number of employees and your own priority number. Add a line for the secretary's name. Once you have compiled all of your cards, you need to prioritize where you want to work.

Sample Card
Industry Name
Hiring Authority (Name)
Address
Telephone#
Secretaries Name
Product Line

Major Places of Operation

#Of Employees
Cover Letter and Resume sent (Date)
Follow up call - (Date)
Remarks

Monday will be your workday in the office (your home). A cover letter will be prepared for each specific company that will be sent the resume. It is easier to send out ten this week, then ten the next week until the list has been exhausted. In our cover letter in paragraph three, we advised that we would call the next Monday to see if an interview had been arranged. The Monday after the first mailing, we complete the second mailing of ten more packages and then it is on to the telephone. A script that you had practiced would be very handy here. Also try and catch the secretary's name. If you possibly can get the secretary's name on any of your calls, record it on the card. Knowing the secretary by her first name may be your way in the door for an interview and that is your goal.

"Sandy, I'm John Doe and last week I sent a cover letter and resume to Mr. Jones to see if an interview can be arranged to talk about future job opportunities. Has he given you a date for an appointment?"

Now be ready to be rejected. It is going to happen more times than you are ready to hear, but simply and politely state "Thank you, Sandy, I'll check with you next Monday." You may also get rejected by letter but you must keep trying. If you get the interview, record the time and get out your Time Management Chart (page 30). **DO NOT BACK INTERVIEWS INTO ONE-HOUR SLOTS**. Allow for one in the morning and one in the afternoon if they are in the same city. If they are in different areas, allow for one interview only per day.

During the rest of the week prepare cover letters, check newspapers, check in with the same counselor at the Employment Office or One Stop Center, do some informational interviews, check the internet, do more research on companies, check the local library for newspapers from other cities in your area, and get involved with some volunteer activity. The later is an excellent source of leads for employment. The thought there is if you would work that hard for nothing, how much harder you would work for pay. This also can help your psychological clock stay in balance during this stressful time.

Monday morning it is back into the office to restart the same procedures. Stay organized and positive and you will get that interview.

Job Development is hard working but by applying your energy full-time to the many tasks of research, cover letters, mailings, checklists, prepared scripts and telephone contacts, you will be a success.

Chapter VI
THE INTERVIEW

The interview is one of the most important meetings in your life. You are literally selling yourself. How well you do will depend on how well you have prepared and practiced. The interview could easily start on the telephone when you call in to make or get the appointment. How well you are perceived during this conversation could set the future tone for the rest of the interview process. You can help this interview process with some preparation.

Know yourself and be able to talk about you. What are your interests, aptitude, qualifications and your hobbies? Make sure your hobbies are action oriented or constructive in nature. Once again, TV watching is out.

You have already done research on the company during the job development phase and have it available in your 3" X 5" card file. Review this prior to the interview.

Conservative appearance is the name of the game for an interview. No frills, excessive jewelry, flashy tie, sports clothes, or untrimmed hair. Don't chew gum or smoke during the interview. Nails need to be clean and use a mouthwash. No odorous aftershave, colognes or body perfume.

Go to the interview alone and plan to arrive at least ten minutes early. This will give you the opportunity to read any company literature and at the same time make you feel more comfortable with your surroundings. If you haven't previously sent a resume, give one to the secretary to attach to your interview package. You may have to go much earlier if you have to fill out an application. Check with the secretary to see what is required.

Your big moment has arrived. The door is open to the Director's office and you are ushered in. Remember a negative first impression cannot be erased by a thirty-minute interview so it must be all positive. You can destroy it all on the handshake. Your hand should join the interviewer's hand all the way to where the thumb meets the hand. That firmness will not hurt any arthritis that could be in the fingers. Do not sit until asked by the interviewer.

Body language is now the key. You must sit alert in the chair maintaining good eye contact. If you have trouble with eye contact, stare at the bridge of the nose. This eye contact portrays honesty which we learned every employer is looking for. While sitting in the chair, do not cross your legs. This portrays a closed person not interested in what the interviewer has to say. Make sure you remember the interviewer's name.

Team Interviews

Many companies are using team interviews in order to comply with equal opportunity guidelines and the fact that in many cases you could be working with this team on the job. The basic procedures are still the same even though you feel this is an interrogation by a group. At the end of the interview, they will compare notes to get the best person for the job. Many teams will use a process of decision analysis, where all interview questions are graded and a score can be arrived at to objectively make a wise selection.

Interviewers use fairly standard questions that you need to rehearse, but not memorize. Try them in front of a mirror at home while maintaining eye contact with yourself.

- Tell me a little about yourself.
- What can we do for you today?
- What position are you applying for?
- What made you choose our company?
- Why did you choose this particular career?
- What is your most important accomplishment in your life to date?
- What are your dreams (short & long range goals)?
- What is your greatest weakness?
- What is your greatest strength?
- What did you like most/least about school?
- What have you done that shows initiative?
- What have you done that shows leadership?
- What is your definition of success?

- Are you qualified for this job?
- Why should I hire you?

It would be illegal for an employer to inquire about a job seeker's marital status, sex, age, race, color, religion, national origin, arrest record or any physical or mental disabilities during the interview process or prior to an offer of employment.

Never argue with the interviewer and never criticize former employers or co-workers. Don't apologize for lack of experience, but instead, stress your strong points and how this will carry you on the new job. This is not a counseling session so never bring up problems at home. You would be automatically put in that 5% category.

You can ask some questions that are pertinent to the job you are applying for.

- What kind of person do you hope to hire for this job?
- What would a typical day's duties be like?
- Does the company promote from within?

Stay away from pay and benefits, as they will be told to you before you accept the offer.

When the interview is over, thank the interviewer by name, smile and with a firm handshake, leave the premises. You have no reason to be hanging around. Besides, you have to get to your "office" to write a thank you note. This note is also three paragraphs. The first paragraph will thank them for their time, the second will express continued interest in the job or your desire to withdraw from consideration and the third will be any additional information you left out during the interview. You will additionally add them to your Monday morning telephone call list. Hopefully it will end with a job offer.

Chapter VII
THE JOB OFFER

Generally the job offer will not come until the second or third interview. When you researched your career in Chapter One, you found a salary range for your particular profession. If you scanned the computer at the Employment Office or the One Stop Center, you found out what the job was paying locally. In "The Occupational Outlook Handbook," you found a range of $16,000 to $30,000 per year for an Electrical Engineering Tech. "Getting Started: North Carolina Jobs and Careers," showed a range of $20,000 to $25,000 per year. The computer at the local Employment Office/Job Link showed $20,500 to $21,500. Let's look at these figures and see what the salary range you would be requesting.

- OOH 16000   30000
- State 20000   25000
- Local 20500   21500

From the diagram and the state figures, the National high would be too much to shoot for. The National low is also out of the range. To make it fit the area and the state, you should start slightly below the area level and use the state upper level as your top. The requested salary would be $21,400 to $25,000. This would fit partly in the employer's range and within your expectations for your career.

Employer	Job Seeker
	25,000
21,500	
	21,400
20,500	

The objective is to satisfy all parties during these critical negotiations.

Benefits also need to be considered during the salary negotiation period.

Benefits traditionally cost between 25% to 30% of your basic salary. They could include vacation, sick leave, retirement, medical, life-dental insurance, etc. Let us assume that company "A" does not have a benefit package and they offer you a flat salary of $18,000 per year. Company "B" has a benefit package that equals 30% of your salary, but they are only going to offer you $15,000 per year.

Salary Offer	18,000	15,000
Benefits	0	4,500
Total Salary	18,000	19,500

Not only are you further ahead with company "B" by this comparison, but you are further ahead by paying less taxes. In most cases individuals cannot get the same benefits provided by companies for the same price and with company "A" you will have to pay for it with already taxed dollars. All other things being equal and considering promotion potential, Company "B" would be the ideal choice.

If the student is interested in further initial negotiation discussions on future raises and promotions, you are referred to "What Color is My Parachute." This author does not believe in the "What if" theory but in the accomplishment of tasks and then addressing this proven performance while asking for a raise on a yearly basis only if merited. A raise on merit is not to be confused with a cost of living allowance, which most companies give to adjust for yearly inflation.

You will be starting with Company "B" in one week.

Chapter VIII
IN THE WORLD OF WORK

DAY ONE

While you were interviewing with Company "B", you should have noticed the appearance of the individuals that worked there. That is the way you will dress for the first day on the job. If you have any doubts, be conservative. Report 5 to 10 minutes early on that first workday. The company will assign someone to assist you to get the necessary paperwork accomplished and to give you a brief orientation and introductions to your fellow employees. Even on this day you are not there to socialize, but to work. You can't start long conversations with your fellow employees because they are at work.

You will need your social security number as issued by the Federal Government. The five-dollar card that you can buy commercially will not replace the Government Issue due to the fact you must prove citizenship. You will probably need an additional picture identification card. Have a pen and pencil with you, as you will be asked to fill out many forms before you actually start in your new job.

If you don't see a job description during the interview, you will need to obtain one during the orientation process. This job description should tell you who you work for, and what your duties and responsibilities are.

You also need to know where you and others fit in the structure of the organization. Most companies will have a chart in their personnel or procedure manual. The rules and procedures can be found in a handbook that will be given to you during your in processing or orientation. Don't just throw it in your drawer. Read it from cover to cover and get an explanation from your boss or a team member on anything you do not understand. This can save you from embarrassment, discipline, or even firing at a later date.

You have entered at the bottom of the world of work in your organization. Everyone wants to succeed in his or her job, but how is it done? Your blueprint is following the a, b, c's.

Period "A" can last from 4 hours to one week as you process into the company. "B" is a training period that can last from a day to several months in duration. Every organization will teach you your job their way. Don't forget "Their way", not your way. Your attitude during this period will be a big part of your fitting into the corporate picture. You are severely judged on behavior, positive attitude, promotional potential, abilities, dependability, and especially absenteeism. In period "C" You are on your own gathering experience. It will be noted by your supervisor and your fellow team members how well you work without supervision and the amount of work you produce.

Your results during period "C" has been tremendous and nine months after entering the company, you are promoted to head the section. Congratulations! Now what?

You definitely have what is called promotion potential. You are now in period "D". You can do a good job and stay comfortably as a section head for the rest of your life or you can set goals for advancement for yourself. Hopefully you choose the latter.

What are these new goals? Number one will be continuing education, known now as life long learning. Many CEO's have referred to education as the heart of a company's success. This can be accomplished through formal education classes taught at local colleges or universities. Seminars and workshops will add to your knowledge. You must learn the management skills of:

> Supervising
> Communicating
> Organizing
> Delegating
> Decision Making
> Budgeting.
> Team Development

You may be able to get some basics by checking with your library for videotapes on these subjects that do a good job in a short session. Observe other supervisors and team members and pick and choose those attributes and traits you want to retain. Don't be afraid to ask for advice of those that appear to be on the ladder of advancement.

You may be asked to represent your organization in Civic or Service Clubs. In these organizations, you promote the image of your company and at the same time serve the community that you work in. This is an excellent opportunity to build leadership skills as you work on committees and eventually chair them and move into the leadership roles that your company wants you to have both in the community and in the work setting.

Professional organizations will allow for the same type of leadership experiences as well as allowing you to keep your professional and technical skills up to speed.

ASSERTIVENESS

Are you passive? Are you aggressive? Neither one of these traits will help you climb that ladder of success. Assertiveness can help you achieve the middle ground that you are after. Honest communications is the bedrock of assertiveness. Dr. Manuel Smith has an excellent book on the subject called, "When I Say No I Feel Guilty". This book should be number one on your list not just for the world of work, but for your social and family life as well. Assertiveness can also help you with sexual harassment.

SEXUAL HARASSMENT

What is sexual harassment? The Equal Employment Opportunity Commission's

(EEOC) amended "Guidelines on Discrimination Because of Sex" states:

"Unwelcome sexual advances, requests for sexual favors and other verbal or physical conduct of a sexual nature constitute sexual harassment when any one of these criteria are met:

1. Submission to such conduct is made either explicitly or implicity a term or condition of an individual's employment.

2. Submission to or rejection of such conduct by an individual is used as the basis.

3. Such conduct has the purpose or affect of unreasonably interfering with an individual's work performance or creating an intimidating, hostile or offensive work environment.

Sexual harassment is sexual behavior that is unwelcome and is therefore illegal. It has increased dramatically over the past number of years at a rate of approximately 15% per year. Sexual harassment can be costly to employers and employees either monetarily or in negative work attitudes that can effect employees psychologically or physiologically. Terman (1988)

As the penalties that are awarded by the courts increase, more lawyers will advocate going the court route. You must keep your work environment professional and businesslike. Supervisors can be held responsible for acts committed by their employees even if they didn't have knowledge of the specific act, so maintain the highest level of professionalism respecting everyone's rights.

PAY RAISES
Another type of harassment that can definitely affect you, is when you don't get a pay raise. Most

companies operate for profit and of course any pay raises detract from that profit. In most cases you can count on a COLA (Cost Of Living Allowance) which is given to all employees to keep pace with inflation, but you cannot generally count on a pay raise based on merit unless you ask for it. You need to arm yourself prior to the start of your company's fiscal year with your accomplishments at work and even with those extracurricular activities that you did in the community that promoted the company and you. Don't be excessive in your request as a 3 to 5 percent salary increase over and above COLA is considered outstanding. You will need to rehearse this presentation which you, will give to your supervisor. You should also prepare a summary sheet listing the accomplishments, which you will leave with him or her. Do not get emotional during your presentation for the raise and do not show disappointment or anger if you are turned down. Your boss may know something you don't.

That something he/she may know is that we are in to downsizing or right sizing. Security is not like it used to be when you could count on working thirty years for a company and then retirement would come. To help yourself through these less stable times you need to have a savings account with at least six months of basic living expenses available and also start a 401k plan which will allow you to control your own destiny for your future retirement as this plan can move with you through jobs and career changes.

Good luck in the world of work. I hope the simplification provided by this Workbook will allow for an easy transition into a job whether it is from school, unemployment or change of career. Comments or suggestions are solicited and should be sent to the author. Above all else you need to keep up your positive attitude and don't give up!

REFERENCES

Bolles, R. N. (1987) What Color is Your Parachute? Berkeley: Ten Speed Press.

Bolles, R. N. The Three Boxes of Life, Berkeley: Ten Speed Press.

Burgiss, L. (Ed.) (1987) Getting Started: North Carolina Jobs and Careers. Raleigh: Employment Security Commission.

Dictionary of Occupational Titles (5th ed). (1989) Washington, D.C.: U.S. Department of Labor, Bureau of Labor Statistics.

Occupational Outlook Handbook, (1990-1991 ed.) Washington, D.C.: Department of Labor, Bureau of Labor Statistics.

Standard and Poor's Register of Corporations, Directors, and Executives, 3 Vols. (1982) New York: Standard and Poor's Corporation.

Terman, B. (1988) Making Advances. Deerfield, II: Simon & Schuster.

ABOUT THE AUTHOR

Ed Kelly wrote this book to supplement a class he taught at Wayne Community College in Goldsboro, NC. He found that he spent 75% of his time counseling students on how to get a job on graduation and that it would be more advantageous to teach a course to 30 students at a time. Not being able to find a book that totally spelled out the strategy for employment, he wrote Your Move into the World of Work that lays out in simple steps the requirements necessary for finding that job that you, the job seeker, will be happy with. The author has 40 years of experience in training. He was an instructor navigator in the USAF for over 20 years and as a Director of Cooperative Education, Job Placement and Apprenticeship Training for the community college system. He has conducted state, regional, and national workshops on how to obtain employment. In retirement, he conducts a monthly workshop at Central Florida Community College in Ocala, Florida for those retirees that want to re-enter the workforce. He has a Masters Degree in Education, Guidance and Counseling from Campbell University.